KEMPTON PARK AUTOJUMBLE
MOTORCYCLES AND STUFF

CELEBRATING 30 YEARS

PICTURES BY MAURO CARRARO

KEMPTON PARK AUTOJUMBLE
MOTORCYCLES AND STUFF

CELEBRATING 30 YEARS

CONTENT PAGE

ERIC's STORY

With a family background in steam engines, including a grandfather who drove steamrollers for a living, the event's founder, Eric Patterson, started his working life in hospitals as a steam engine fitter. Some might consider this connection quite apt given his penchant for speed and the inherent danger of his past time!

Eric satisfied his need for speed through motorcycling over many years, on all varieties of motorbikes, before taking on the challenge of the Bonneville Salt Flats in 2008. It was there that he fulfilled one of his lifetime ambitions when he broke the Bonneville land speed record several times on a Norton Jap 1150, finishing with an impressive 121.795mph when the record was only 100mph. He returned a further five times, twice with Brough Superior, achieving more records in 2011 and 2013 and finally, in 2014, gaining two more records on his Vincent Viscount, the best of which was at 131.68mph.

Eric's life-long passion has led him to witness some of motorcycling legends' greatest moments. Watching Geoff Duke race his famous bikes at the Isle of Man TT and Mike Hailwood's glorious comeback win in 1978 are amongst the most memorable. He's even been known to sit swapping stories with the equally ardent and legendary motorcyclist John Surtees.

Like the machines that he has spent a lifetime cherishing, preserving and presenting, Eric, along with his partner Cathy, has made the Kempton Autojumble a legendary and inspirational place for people to keep alive their magnificent classic machines.

KEMPTON AUTOJUMBLE STORY

For over thirty years, Kempton Park Autojumble has been a relative Mecca for a band of motorcycle enthusiasts to gather and exhibit, sell or simply browse the multitude of stalls of vintage motorcycle bric-a-brac, rare gems and sought-after parts that have long since ceased production.

From its humble beginnings in 1978 where founder, Eric Patterson, hired 25 stalls from one Mrs. Pigeon at Eton Town Hall for the princely sum of 25p each, it's concept soon proved popular with local enthusiasts and, after only 2 events, the need for larger premises led to a move to Ascot Racecourse in 1979. With interest and attendance continuing to grow over the following years, it became clear that an even larger dedicated space was required. So, having outgrown the site at Ascot, the move to Kempton Park Racecourse was made in 1986. Building on the autojumble's success, 1988 saw the birth of two special-interest shows, The Southern Classic and The Off-road Racing Show, drawing competitors from across the country to display their beautifully restored and diverse machines to the delight of classic bike enthusiasts.

For many of the classic and vintage motorcycling community, the event acts as a social meeting point in their calendars or simply the chance to catch up. Held seven times a year, the Kempton Park Autojumble is that special place for vintage enthusiasts to indulge their passion for classic machines that are genuine pieces of engineering artistry.

The majority of the motorcycles shown come from an era of British manufacturing when these early machines were at the cutting edge of technology and design innovation. The craftsmanship in the build quality is testament to their durability and popularity. The autojumble has kept alive many a marque that would otherwise have long disappeared.

FOR SALE

1949 Douglas Mk4 350cc

Matching numbers (Engine & Frame)
Original Number Plate

£3,250

The Classic MotorCycle

Red alert
Moto Guzzi racer

Inter Norton
Poland's Harley
Matchless G15 CSR
Enfield Cycar and R...
...ll about plain bea...

87

£5

BSA
1926

Colonial
9.86hp

B.S.A.

32

Early racing in Britain, including meets such as the Isle of Man TT in 1907 and Brooklands in 1908, acted as proving grounds for every new technological idea that made the reputation of these dream machines. Many of these pedigrees still command big premiums.

1893 saw the birth of Royal Enfield, now the world's oldest motorcycle manufacturer in continuous production. Their off-road bikes are still in existence over a hundred and twenty-five years later. From their original use during the First World War by dispatch riders crossing inhospitable terrain, off-roaders and the adventure bikes evolving from them, have caught the imagination of every manufacturer. The most popular of these is the ubiquitous BMW GS series which has been winning accolades for the last few decades.

greevesgriffon380

1969
Lower compression
& de compressor
Wide range gearbox r...
New mains ...
For...

1958 Triumph TR6
Reg No YNX963
Ex I.S.D.T machine

This Triumph TR6 650cc is the ex Triumph factory I.S.D.T machine ridden by John Giles in the 1958 I.S.D.T held in Garmisch Partenkirchen Germany. YNX963 was one of three machines prepared for that years event by the factory and to the best of our knowledge YNX963 is the only surviving machine. John used this same machine in the Welsh 3-day prior to the 1958 event. In the six-day he won a gold medal for the British Trophy team. The present owner has had the machine since 1975 and has restored it to its I.S.D.T condition as it was in a sad condition when first bought it. If you have any information, photo's etc. the owner would be very happy to talk to you.

John Giles on board YNX963 at the start of the 1958 I.S.D.T with H.R.Vaughan Britains team manager.

SOUTHERN OFF ROAD
& RACING SHOW 2014

8

The 1960's saw bikes being customised to resemble TT race wining bikes. Enthusiasts looked to save money and develop their engineering skills in the hope to experience the rush of speed, not always legally, as they raced their machines from coffee bar to coffee bar. The Café racer was born as were races from Chelsea Bridge to the Ace Café and late night breakneck runs to Brighton. Today customising old bikes has become an art form with machines looking like exhibits for an art gallery.

SPEEN STORES

1965
Velocette
Thruxton

499cc -The Ultimate Sports Velocette

The most powerful production Velocette and
this original example was one of the first made.

1988 saw the birth of two special-interest shows, The Southern Classic and The Off-road Racing Show, drawing competitors from across the country to display their beautifully restored and diverse machines. Competitive classes range from Best Club Stand to Best Bike in Show and exhibits vary from small, never to be seen again manufacturers to pristine factory race replicas, all lovingly restored to their former glory. Some would even go so far as to say that they are better than when they originally came out of the factory.

... self-explanatory model assists with the ... understanding of the NSU/Wankel rotary ... combustion engine. The Wankel rotary concept ... later developed and manufactured by NSU ... the 1950s. To form this single rotary display, ... combination of main engine parts are used ... two very different rotary motorcycles. ... trochoid and rotary piston, from a damaged ... cooled DKW, the shaft was cut from a ... liquid cooled Norton rotary twin along with the ... cover. By slowly turning the shaft anti-... clockwise you will see how the stationary and ... rotary gears combine at a 3 to 1 ratio keeping ... the 3 sided piston (without seals) in contact ... with the trochoid surface throughout its orbit. ... This allows you to follow a 4 stroke cycle in ... one piston revolution. This concept is the only ... manufactured rotary prime mover to be used ... commercially throughout the world in variable ... applications and still manufactured today.

For further information please speak to----

Rotary Roy

Kempton Park attracts all sorts of motorcycle enthusiasts, from collectors of classic magazine back issues to bespoke manufacturers of patent British motorcycle parts. The bikes shown are in various states, some fully restored, others in need of serious care and attention. Then there are the truly rare specimens. They all have their own unique quality that sets them apart from the other bikes of their era, making them classic.

BIKE FOR SALE
Kempton Park Autojumble July 23, 2016

Make: TRIUMPH
Model: THUNDERBIRD 6T 1953
Price: 13,500
Tel: 07768834646
USA IMPORT

BIKE FOR SALE

Kempton Park Autojumble July 23, 2016

Make:

Model:

Price:

Tel:

You can trace the bloodline for today's modern motorcycles through the evolution of these most successful machines, some of which are still in production today with almost identical evolutionary technology. The latest incarnations may have had to conform to European Legislation and Safety Compliancy but their origins are unmistakeable. Kempton keeps alive the original elements of innovation, excitement and danger that stirs the imagination and feeling that motorcycling is a pastime for bad boys and girls.

107

European bikes have either been eye-wateringly beautiful or effective and efficient machines. They've been ridden by most of the famous names in the motorcycling world and catch the imagination of every enthusiast. At Kempton, they are often the reddest, the raciest, the most stylish or simply the most comfortable and reliable. Without doubt, they are the ones that attract the most attention. Like all pedigrees, they come with their quirks but one thing you can guarantee is that they have been designed to be looked at as much as ridden.

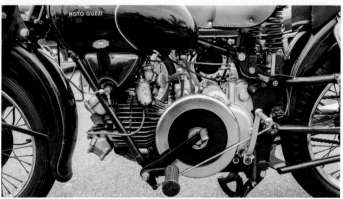

In 1959 Mr. Soichiro Honda decided to enter the most prestigious motorcycle race at the time, The Isle of Man TT. This little known Japanese manufacturer appeared with a clutch of 125s and finished the fortnight with some strong results. By 1961 they were winning all the trophies, sealing Honda's reputation for daringly engineered slick bikes. They still dominate the TT and many of today's racing competitions. Their early machines are now becoming classics in their own right.

IMAGE CREDITS

Riding motorcycles has been a lifelong passion that started in my early teens, although I wasn't allowed to ride on the road till I was 16. Once I hit that milestone, that's when my whole world changed. Like most bikers, riding a bike has always been about freedom, adventure and risk taking for me, all the things a young teenager thrives on and parents hope you will outgrow. Unfortunately for them, this didn't happen.

I'm a UK based rider and most of my world revolves around family, friends and occasionally work! Motorbikes and bike riding takes up much of the rest of it. Every day I wake up and my first thought is "what's the weather going to be like?". With the exception of the bleak wintry weather, I try to ride in all seasons as that way each day starts with a new adventure. Having learned the hard way from too many spills in the rain and dark as a young rider, perhaps the self-preservation instinct has finally kicked in.

My other great lifelong passion is photography and indulging them both make for my best days out. Robert Pirsig said it best in Zen and the Art of Motorcycle Maintenance: "You're completely in contact with it all. You're in the scene, not just watching it anymore, and the sense of presence is overwhelming."

Mauro Carraro
Biker-Photographer

ACKNOWLEDGEMENTS

A very special thanks to Eric and Catherine Patterson for all their time and knowledge
in helping compile this book. Aris for his stylish designs. Ian Hatton at Verralls.
Roy at Bullet motorcycles. Andrew Kitchen at Mortons. Ubaldo Sosso at Grafiche Antiga.
And my partner Paloma Casey for putting up with all the Saturdays at Kempton.
Then in editing this book, which I know at times has been quite infuriating
with my constant changes.
Thank you all, your help has been invaluable.

Official Sponsors Bohnams Auctions Bond Street London

First published in 2018 - MCP Pictures and Print
Cover picture: Café Racers Line up for 2015 Southern Classic
All Photographs by Mauro Carraro ©
Text by Mauro Carraro and Paloma Casey ©
Designed by Aris Akritidis
Images cannot be reproduced without permission of the owner
All rights reserved

Mauro Carraro has asserted his right under the Copyright,
Design and Patents Act to be identified as the author of this work.

Printed in Italy by Grafiche Antiga

www.maurocarrarophotography.com